I MET A MAN WITH A SHINING FACE
An Autobiography in the Things of God

by
HARRY E. JESSOP, D.D.
Dean of Chicago Evangelistic Institute

AUTHOR OF
Foundations of Doctrine in Scripture and Experience
The Holiness People
That Burning Question of Final Perseverance
When Prayer Seems Not to Work

SCHMUL PUBLISHING COMPANY
NICHOLASVILLE, KENTUCKY

Published by Schmul Publishing Co.
PO Box 776
Nicholasville, KY USA

Printed in the United States of America

ISBN 10: 0-88019-209-7
ISBN 13: 978-0-88019-209-5

Visit us on the Internet at www.wesleyanbooks.com, or order direct from the publisher by calling 800-772-6657, or by writing to the above address.

Contents

Dedicated to
"The Man With The Shining Face"

and to
Every other radiant soul
who by a sunlit countenance
makes others desire the blessing they enjoy.

Foreword

THE PAGES WHICH FOLLOW embody a story which I have long desired to write. Its very nature has made it necessary for me to employ the first person singular, hence the constant use of the capital I which may seem to protrude. In using it, the only desire has been to explain a personal experience and thereby magnify the Lord Jesus who alone has performed this soul-renewing work. The I, we trust, is the crucified I of Galatians 2:20; not the carnal I of Luke 18:11, 12.

—H.E.J.

Chicago, Illinois, 1941

"And when he came down from the mount Moses wist not that the skin of his face shone while he talked with him."

"And the children of Israel saw the face of Moses, that the skin of Moses' face shone." Ex. 34:29, 35.

Section I

THIS IS MY STORY

"Come and hear, all ye that fear God, and I will declare what God hath done for my soul." Psalm 66:16.

1
RELATING THE INCIDENT

I MET A MAN with a shining face—and I mean really shining. It was a face having upon it the glow of heaven and the glory of God.

Let there be no mistake about it, my language is not mystical; I am not thinking about the face of Moses as described in the Scriptures, neither am I speaking of the face of the Lord Jesus beheld by the eye of faith in contemplative meditation, true though it be that "God, who commanded the light to shine out of darkness, hath shined in our hearts, to give the light of the knowledge of the glory of God in the face of Jesus Christ." 2 Cor. 4:6.

The face was the face of a man; a man of my own generation; a young man, probably not more than ten years my senior. Only a few years before this incident he had entered the Christian ministry and because of his unswerving loyalty to a newly-discovered spiritual experience to which he declared he must testify, he had met the full force of an unexpected blast of ecclesiastical opposition issuing from a church board composed of men ready to fight for things they considered fundamental, yet without any notion concerning the deep things of God.

They were determined that their church should not be disturbed by this *young upstart* who was daring to preach such radical notions among them.

To the amazement of all concerned, the opposition did not *silence* him, and to their further amazement, their persecution did not *sour* him. When he was denounced he did not fight back, and when evicted he quietly withdrew. On being told that in view of his *heresy* the church could no longer support him, neither would the pulpit be open further for his ministry, he launched out into a life of faith, preaching, like Wesley, wherever an opening could be found and trusting God to meet his needs. This God did in a marvelous way.

The opposition drove him deeper, and still deeper into God, until on his countenance as naturally as his own complexion, there shone the radiance which I have described.

My first meeting with this man was in the month of May, 1906, and, little as I dreamed it then, that meeting was destined to prove the crossroad which was to lead to the settling of one of the greatest issues of my life.

Certainly I needed to meet somebody, for spiritually I had a deep-rooted need. I had known the Lord Jesus in saving power for more than five years. My conversion had been intensely real. It was so very definite that I knew the date. It had produced an incontrovertible testimony which I found it a delight to give. I knew I had been born again. It happened on the last Sunday of January, 1901, about four o'clock in the afternoon. That day I had come into personal contact with Jesus Christ and had received my pardon at His hand. I passed from death unto life; the Spirit's witness came into my heart.

So real and definite was all this that all who knew me became aware of the marked change that had taken place. From that moment to the time at which I now write, the fact of my salvation has never once been in doubt.

Yet I was puzzled—sadly puzzled. Somehow, within my

experience, Scripture and the practical outworkings did not agree. Certainly I could find isolated verses, which taken from their context and separated from their historical setting, would for the moment silence my heart cry and condone my defeat, but my trouble was that my heart cry would not remain silenced, and when I honestly faced my defeats in my Lord's presence in the place of prayer, I was utterly ashamed.

I had only little knowledge at that time concerning the laws of Bible exegesis, yet I felt within my soul that those verses—often only parts of verses—so often emphasized by my religious teachers in support of their "must sin every day in thought, word and deed" theory, did not represent full-orbed Bible truth, and that such a theory was not worthy of the price my Lord had paid for my redemption. There were other Scriptures which, to say the least, did not emphasize that phase, and although at the time the thought seemed so strangely contradictory, I became increasingly conscious that somewhere there must be a key which as yet I had not found.

Among the numerous Scripture passages which troubled me was Paul's magnificent declaration, "Nay, in all these things we are more than conquerors through him that loved us." Romans 8:37. When I honestly faced such a declaration, I knew that my experience did not match it. Not that I ever hoped to match it in the things which this mighty warrior of the Cross actually endured, but I felt very definitely that God expected me to be as gloriously triumphant in my circumstances as Paul had been in his.

When at length I ventured to voice such a thought among my religious associates, they insisted that I was taking the Bible far too literally. It did not mean, they declared, that we could be conquerors in *everything* but in *things in general.* To make the Bible apply to every detail was going too far. "And yet," they went on to say, "in reality you are more than conqueror, because Christ is the conqueror and you are in Him. You, of course, are always failing but all the time *His victory* is put to *your account.* He conquered on Calvary, and even though every day you may fall and be defeated, you are credited with *what He has done*, not with *what you are doing*, therefore in the sight of God, defeated as you are, you are *more than conqueror.*"

Frankly I did not know what to make of it. It seemed to me that if this was the best God had to offer, Christ and Calvary were set to condone rather than to conquer. It did not seem to make sense, and certainly it did not bring glory to God. The more I thought and prayed about it, the more puzzled I became.

It was during this time of spiritual perplexity that I met my friend with the shining face, and by that period God had graciously prepared me for the meeting. I shall always believe that just as definitely as Philip was sent to meet the eunuch by the way of Gaza and Paul was directed to the disciples at Ephesus, that man was divinely placed in my path that day. How that face did shine! If my own experience perplexed me, that face perplexed me more. It betokened an evident satisfaction, for it radiated a rare spiritual glow. Young and inexperienced as I was in the things of God, I could detect the difference between this spiritual *glow* and a natural *grin*. But how had that glow of spiritual satisfaction come there? What deep divine secret had he found?

Then came my second surprise; it was in the form of a question. It became evident that the interest was not all on one side; that while I had been studying him, he, too, had been studying me, and had rightly appraised my inward need. It seemed as though he had been looking down into the deep places of my spiritual nature, had seen my emptiness and recognized my hunger.

"Brother," said he, "have *you* been baptized with the Holy Ghost and fire?" To say the question surprised me would be to put it mildly indeed. I was startled; almost stunned. A later contemplation of that hour has seemed to bring a comparison with the incident of Paul and the Ephesian disciples as recorded in Acts 19:1-7. Acknowledging their present experience, yet recognizing their apparent lack, he inquired, "Have ye received the Holy Ghost since ye believed?" So puzzled were these men that in their perplexity they stammered out, "We have not so much as heard whether there be any Holy Ghost." It could hardly be that they were entirely unaware of the existence of the third Person of the Trinity; surely Apollos, their pastor, had at least taught them that. What they seem to be saying is exactly what I said to my questioner nearly nineteen centuries later, when hardly knowing how to frame my reply, I said, "I don't know what you mean by being baptized with the Holy Ghost and fire, but if that is it that shines on your face, I want it."

He then began to tell me his story, the substance of which was as follows:

"There was a time when I was as hungry hearted as you are today, but I did not know what it was I was hungry for. Following my ordination I had gone to my first church, a keen young minister with lots in my head but with a heart that was becoming lean and dry. My sermons were intellectual and were, I fear, designed to *please* rather than to *convict*. After some weeks of my ministry, I was met at the foot of the pulpit stairs one Sunday morning by a queer little woman—at least that was my estimate of her at the time—who shook my hand cordially, smiled at me sweetly, and then amazed me by saying, 'Young man, that was a very clever sermon you preached this morning, but do you know you are as blind as a bat? I am praying for you'; and before I had time to recover from my astonishment she had disappeared.

"Now whether that old lady showed the best judgment in the way she approached me, might of course provide a subject for discussion. Certainly I was not flattered by her remark and I did not fail to show it. It is not to my credit when I say I began to make pointed remarks in my sermons especially for her benefit, and for these later I found it necessary to make an open apology. The thing that puzzled me, however, was that she never argued with me. The more cutting my remarks became the more she beamed, and each time she met me she greeted me with a warm 'God bless you! I am praying for you,' and much as I hated to acknowledge it, I knew deep down in my heart that *the queer old lady*, as I had chosen to call her, possessed something to which I was a total stranger.

"At last I could bear it no longer, and going to her with my hungry heart, I asked her to forgive me, pray for me, and tell me the secret of her radiant experience. She told me that since the first day I entered the church she had prayed and intended to continue as long as I remained. Then looking me straight in the eyes she asked, 'Did you ever hear about the Second Blessing?' 'No!' I replied, 'I have never heard of it. What is it?' 'Well,' said she, 'it is what John Wesley preached; what the Bible teaches; and what I've got. Everybody ought to have it, and God wants you to have it.' I asked the old lady to pray that God would give me that experience. She did; I began to pray for it myself; I placed all I had on the altar of consecration and God met my need. Thank God I have the Blessing today."

As I stood in that humble Yorkshire home, the earnestness of spirit in my new-found friend and the evident satisfaction he enjoyed only made me hunger the more. For the first time in my life I felt I was looking into the face of a man who really knew God and found complete satisfaction in Him. He did not seek to press me into any undue acceptance of doctrine, but with an earnestness that was deep and meaningful he said, "And brother, God can do the same thing for you." He invited me to attend a holiness convention to be held in the city two days later and then said good-bye.

The following Thursday found me attending my first holiness convention. The afternoon service only tended to increase my hunger and my determination to have that hunger satisfied.

I remained between meetings for tea and fellowship. I was not at ease, for I did not know what to talk about. These men seemed to live in a realm to which I was a stranger; they talked about things which bewildered me. To them God seemed to be so intensely real. The Bible was a book which they seemed to think had been written especially for their benefit. They talked about the promises God had given them; about things they had been led to do, and so on.

At last my poor carnal heart began to manifest itself. These brethren did not seem to recognize that *I, too*, was a preacher—only a local preacher at that time, but a *preacher* none the less. It was time I said something, so looking at the one who seemed to be the leader I asked, "What do you think is the best commentary for a preacher to use?" And without moving an eyelid, he replied, "Why don't you try the Holy Ghost?" I have often wondered whether I looked as small as I felt. My face reddened. I felt myself shrivel up inside. Poor, proud little peacock that I was, something like that was what I needed. I had been petted and pampered and made to feel my full size by indulgent church officials, who were anxious to keep their young people, yet in their ignorance were going the wrong way about it, but here were men who were not willing to minister to my carnal pride, and God was using them to make me see how small I really was.

That night David Thomas, a London drygoods dealer, preached. *Preached*, did I say? Measured by canons of homiletics it was a poor sermon indeed. Evidently he was not a trained preacher, but as I learned afterward, a business man who delighted to give both time and money to the proclamation of Full Salvation truth. Yet whatever may be said of his *sermon*, there was no doubt about his message. It would have been a very dull member of that congregation who missed what he was trying to say. He preached with an unction which betokened a divine indwelling. There was something about both message and messenger which only the fact of an indwelling God could explain.

The message was based on Acts 1:8, "But ye shall receive power, after that the Holy Ghost is come upon you; and ye shall be witnesses unto me..." The Holy Ghost! It thrilled my soul to hear this man use the term. The Holy Ghost! He was to come upon me! To possess me! To use me! It seemed too good to be true, and yet God's Word said it, therefore it must be true.

That night found me kneeling as a seeker at the altar of prayer and that night God sanctified me wholly. I began by asking for power; it was the best I knew; but by the baptism with the Holy Ghost and fire God destroyed indwelling sin, and from that night onward I was never the same man again.

2
DESCRIBING WHAT FOLLOWED

THE DAYS WHICH FOLLOWED were far beyond anything I had anticipated in power and blessing. Certainly the powers of darkness very definitely withstood my claim and God put my faith to the test, but soon in a very real sense it was evident that the Holy Ghost had taken complete possession of my soul. Since that time thirty-five years have passed, but I have never had reason to change my mind concerning what was then done, nor to doubt the nature of the experience wrought.

Such an experience has often been criticized because of its suddenness. "Is it not something in the nature of a flash in the pan?" "Do these *flashes* really last?" "Would it not be better to seek something more stable?" To all this we reply that the abiding nature of this *flash in the pan* as some may choose to call it, depends first of all, if we may continue the use of the figure, on the nature of the *flash*, and further, upon the *pan*.

It will be well then to make sure as to the nature of the *flash* — everything depends on that. If it is merely a wave of *emotion*, then just as quickly as it came, so quickly will it subside. If, however, it is the work of an Almighty God, its results will surely remain. Paul indicated this when he wrote:

> "And the very God of peace sanctify you wholly; and I pray God your whole spirit and soul and body be preserved blameless unto the coming of our Lord Jesus Christ. Faithful is he that calleth you, who also will do it." 1 Thess. 5:23, 24.

It will further depend on the *attitude* of the soul receiving the flash. The Blessing thus bestowed is not independent and self-sustaining, but relative, and can only be retained in relation to and in humble dependence on its Author, God Himself.

It became necessary, however, quite early in this new experience to distinguish between God's abiding Blessing and my own fluctuating feelings. I had no delusions about the fact that although sanctified wholly, I still lived in a human body, in a sinful world, and within constant range of satanic attack. It was evident that I must live, not in the realm of feelings, but in the sphere of faith. I was conscious of the enjoyment of a real spiritual fact, and I settled it in my thinking that spiritual facts did not, without definite reason change over night; therefore, my sanctification was not governed by my *feelings*, but by my faith.

Two outstanding thoughts might well be considered here:

(1)

WHAT THE EXPERIENCE BROUGHT TO ME.

My first consciousness was that of *inward purity*. I was immediately aware of a very real cleansing in the depths of my nature. If I may be permitted to state it exactly as I felt it, it seemed as though inwardly I had been given the luxury of a hot bath. And after all, why should not this be so? Is it not reasonable that God should certify His work? In my simplicity I stated what had happened, and soon discovered how scriptural my consciousness had been:

"And God, which knoweth the hearts, bare them witness, giving them the Holy Ghost, even as he did unto us; and put no difference between us and them, purifying their hearts by faith." Acts 15:8, 9.

On discovering this verse, it did not require a lengthy meditation to convince me that it contained a definite four-fold statement which is as follows:

a. The baptism with the Holy Ghost is for all believers. "Giving them the Holy Ghost even as he did unto us."
b. The baptism with the Holy Ghost purifies the heart. "Giving them the Holy Ghost… purifying their hearts."
c. The baptism with the Holy Ghost is received by faith. "… by faith."
d. The baptism with the Holy Ghost brings a distinctive witness. "God… bare them witness…"

This consciousness of my *purification* was now as clear and as real as the previous consciousness of my *pollution* had been. I knew that God had made me inwardly clean. When I say this, those who have participated in this glorious experience will know exactly what I mean, while as for others, it would be useless to argue, seeing that perception of things spiritual is only made possible through personal participation.

I was conscious that this fiery purging had removed something. Let critical minds dissect it as they will, there was a definite liberation from what had been a decided overweight within my humanity. I knew no better way to describe it than to state that the *body of sin* had been *destroyed*.

I was also conscious of a *personal divine indwelling*. My Lord not only cleansed the temple but also took complete possession of all its chambers, or shall I say, it was in the very act of taking possession that the cleansing took place.

It would not be correct to say that prior to this time there had not been any conscious sense of the inward presence of Deity. From that glorious moment when I was born again, the divine life had been there, but there had been very evident hindrances; the Lord was not on the throne. Now, however, it seemed as though all subversive presences had been expelled and my heart had become the place,

> "Where only Christ is heard to speak;
> Where Jesus reigns alone."

Further, I became conscious of a *new enablement.* The promise was, "Ye shall receive power, after that the Holy Ghost is come upon you." Acts 1:8.

I knew the Holy Ghost had come upon me, and in my simplicity, simply because God said so, I expected to have power. My testimony is that God kept His word. I had been told to— RECEIVE— RECOGNIZE— RELY; I did, and I found that it worked.

But let me be more explicit concerning this *power*. It was not something *spectacular*, it was in reality an *enablement*. There were times when it was not even a conscious energizing. Often there came the feeling of extreme weakness but withal a confidence that God would be my strength. As the Holy Spirit has guided, I have gone *in this my might* and God has never failed me, no matter what the task.

There has been something about this enduement which has been so natural as to make it seem quite ordinary. Its coming brought nothing spectacular. With it came neither hurricane sound, a fiery sight, nor languages not my own. It was simply a reinforcement of my spiritual nature by a power that was divine. It was not something seen upon me as a sort of *extra*, but a supernatural naturalness, if I may so express it, manifesting itself something like the fragrance of a rose, and in such a manner that brought glory not to me, but to God. As I preached, God worked in a new way, bringing conviction to needy hearts.

At the same time I began to enjoy a *very gracious sense of personal victory.*

My failure had been chiefly in the home, and there above all places, I wanted to be kind, but something within me had thwarted this again and again. Then my circumstances bothered me. Little things brought irritation and my conduct made me ashamed. The declaration of Romans 8:37 made me feel that this should not be. My new experience brought the longed-for alteration.

Also I found a *deep inward illumination.*

So far as I was concerned some illumination was certainly needed. As an example of this the following will be sufficient indication. The church in which I had been brought up was distinctly postmillennial in its doctrine, although at that time I knew nothing of the controversy between *post* and *pre*; in fact, it had never occurred to me that there might possibly be another point of view. I knew nothing of the expected appearing of the Lord Jesus for His people, never having heard a sermon, read a tract, nor having been given a hint that this might be so. The theologies I had been given to study were postmillennial and even then were limited in their eschatology. I had therefore a confused idea of some sort of a General Judgment after the world had come to an end, but that of course might be millions of years away. All those splendid New Testament passages which teach so plainly the fact of His coming were interpreted as having to do with death. For example:

"Be ye also ready: for in such an hour as ye think not the Son of man cometh." Matthew 24:44.

"I will come again, and receive you unto myself." John 14:3.

These, and other passages, were used as texts for funeral services, and no one ever suggested the possibility of another interpretation.

As soon as the Holy Spirit took possession, my New Testament began to re-interpret itself. I saw that the coming of Jesus would be personal and that these Scriptures had to do with His appearing in the air for His waiting people. I had no human teacher on this subject, but the truth began to stand out wherever I read. Frankly, I was startled, and for the moment was afraid I might be going off into some kind of error. I therefore sought out my friend with the shining face and his associates and found to my astonishment that they, too, knew this truth; in fact, they told me it was a precious teaching cherished by Christ's waiting people through the centuries. Thus, the Holy Spirit enlightened my ignorance, teaching me in the stillness of my own heart what no other man about me seemed to know. Since that day, of course, many volumes have been read on this precious theme, but concerning its beginning in my own thinking, I can honestly say:

"I neither received it of man, neither was I taught it, but by the revelation of Jesus Christ." Galatians 1:12.

I entered into a *new prayer life.*

It was new in more than one sense. I now had a definite longing to pray and as I prayed, I had power to prevail. My prayer vision widened and took in enlarged horizons. My enemies were remembered and blessing was sought on those who opposed me. The heathen world, the cold, worldly church, the godless masses— all became a burden at the Throne of Grace.

Three distinct aspects of the prayer life now developed: I began to develop a *subterranean prayer stream*—I know not what else to call it—a spiritual underflow; a spirit contact; now in a very real sense I knew something of prayer without ceasing. Mighty answers began to manifest themselves; I learned to do business with Deity.

This life of prayer had another aspect, that of *deep divine communion.* I knew what it was to have audience with God and was deeply conscious of the Holy Presence when I prayed.

I found also a phase of prayer beginning to develop about which hitherto I had known nothing, and which at first caused me some surprise. It was that phase which I have since learned to designate as *spirit conflict*. There were times when though free in my own spirit, I became conscious of a peculiar spirit antagonism. At first it concerned me, for after such an outstanding experience of spiritual liberty, I had not expected this battle, especially when I prayed. It was not easy to analyze, but I was very conscious that these conflicts were directed against me rather than being waged within me. It was not the conflict of the old days, that wearisome battle continually waged inside. Now, the keener the conflict the more conscious I became of my deep inward rest.

It was not long before I found a complete explanation for this. My Bible indicated two very different kinds of conflict, one within the unsanctified believer occasioned by the presence of indwelling sin, called also *the flesh*, and the other directed against the sanctified soul by demon powers in the spiritual realm. These two phases of conflict were described by the Apostle Paul in two contrasted verses:

The conflict of the unsanctified soul:

"For the flesh lusteth against the Spirit, and the Spirit against the flesh: and these are contrary the one to the other: so that ye cannot do the things that ye would." Galatians 5:17.

The conflict of the sanctified soul:

"For we wrestle not against flesh and blood, but against principalities, against powers, against the rulers of the darkness of this world, against spiritual wickedness in high places. (Literally: against the spiritual hosts of wickedness in the heavenly realms). Ephesians 6:12.

Another view of these contending hosts is found in Daniel 10:1-14, where for three whole weeks Daniel had to stand in faith until heaven broke through.

I remembered also that it was after the Lord Jesus Himself had received the oncoming Holy Spirit in the Jordan river, that He was "led up of the Spirit into the wilderness to be tempted of the devil." Matthew 4:1. There seemed to be something analogous here. It was necessary that these spiritual forces should be stubbornly withstood.

Then came *weights* of spirit which also at first were puzzling. They did not seem to be related to my own experience and yet they came upon me, never, however, affecting my access to God. I soon saw that *conflict* was not necessarily *condemnation*, and that a weighted spirit did not necessarily concern my personal experience. I had entered into a wider sphere than at first I realized, and becoming divinely sensitized in spirit contact, I was more closely related to other kindred spirits than I knew. Having been brought into definite union with my Lord, I had also come into a mystical union with every other soul who shared that same fellowship. I was now a member of His body, of His flesh and of his bones. Ephesians 5:30. Seeing that "whether one member suffer, all the members suffer with it" (1 Corinthians 12:26), there was a sense in which in proportion to the soul's ability to enter into it, burdens could be carried and suffering borne. I began to rejoice, therefore, in any little privilege to help fill up that which is behind of the sufferings of Christ for His body's sake, whether it had to do with afflictions in the flesh or pressure in the spirit. Colossians 1:24; 2 Corinthians 3:8-18.

I now realized that my prayer life must not be spasmodic. If I was to continue this precious life in God, I could only do it as I maintained a consistent life of prayer. I began to spend nights in prayer, setting apart the Saturday night of each week, which at that time seemed most convenient, for this purpose. After every night of prayer I was conscious of a day of special power and a sense of a new vitality which more than compensated for lack of sleep. There was withal, a peculiar unction upon my preaching. Thus the experience developed within my soul and the deep things of God were increasingly unveiled.

With all this, there burned *an intensified desire to be like Jesus.*

Likeness to my Lord became the supreme concern of my life. It was not enough to be able to talk about a *new experience*—I must *express Him*. This thought now became a passion. I was now His representative, I must therefore be like Him and be so wholly yielded, that through me He might manifest His beauty to a dying world. Just how far I have succeeded only my Lord can say. My daily concern is that I might express Him better, and that now familiar chorus is daily my prayer:

> "Let the beauty of Jesus be seen in me,
> All His wonderful passion and purity;
> O thou Spirit Divine, all my nature refine,
> Till the beauty of Jesus be seen in me."

(2)
WHAT THE EXPERIENCE DEMANDED OF ME.

When I say *demanded* of me, the word used is not one whit too strong. I soon discovered that if I was to retain this Blessing, I must recognize and obey the laws which governed it. Yet while conscious of this as an imperative demand, it was more, for accompanying it, or rather embodied within it, was an *urge*, nay more, an *enabling*. Perhaps instead of saying what the experience *demanded* of me, it would be better to say, what the experience *inspired* within me. Whichever way it is expressed it seemed to be a merging of both.

Among other things five may be mentioned:

It demanded Rigid Separation.
I found that it required as much separation to retain the Blessing as it did to receive it. When I use the word *separation*, I do not mean that disgusting pharisaical thing which criticizes every healthful exercise, insists on young people dressing like grandma, and puts sinful labels on things in themselves harmless and pure.

The fact that some crank has a prejudice against a thing and shouts about it does not thereby make that thing sinful. We must beware lest Satan should draw us off on a sideline magnifying *non-essentials* when we should be stoutly attacking *sin*.

What then is separation? It is nothing more or less than a careful, conscientious walk with God which persistently refuses to deviate a hairsbreadth from the pathway of consecration to anything that would bring a shadow on the spirit or mar the soul's communion with God.

It demanded an Unqualified Declaration.

In other words, a clear, ringing testimony. When our Lord said, "Ye shall receive power... and ye shall be witnesses unto me... ," He was doing more than making a promise that to receive the Holy Spirit would be the enablement for witness bearing; He was declaring the all-time condition of a retained experience, namely, the power to witness and the necessity for letting that power work itself out.

I discovered that as I honored Him with my witness, He honored me with increasing blessing. My soul has been thrilled again and again as I have simply declared my loyalty to Him, and told how He saved me by His grace and sanctified me wholly by the baptism with the Holy Ghost and fire. My observation has been that wherever I have found a soul whose experience has faded out and ultimately has died, a smothered testimony has had something to do with the catastrophe.

Let me again make sure that I am well understood. This declaration is to be more than a pious religious expression and certainly must pass beyond a vague generalization. In my own case I saw that it must be a clear-cut testimony to what God had wrought within me. I saw that it must no longer be *we, us,* and *our;* it must now be *I, me,* and *my.* It is easier to generalize on doctrine than to individualize on experience, that is, if the soul is to be perfectly honest in testimony and keep it up to date.

It should also be noted that a testimony is not a tirade. The man who has nothing better to talk about than the faults of the *other churches* should not call what he has to say a *testimony to holiness*. We are called to witness to the power of our risen Lord in bestowing upon us a *Full Salvation*. That witness must be unqualified and undiluted; without arrogance, yet with a plainness and a precision that makes it impossible for the dullest to misunderstand what we have to say. Such a testimony will always command the blessing of God.

It demanded a Christlike Toleration.

Where and how did that idea arise that it was necessary to be offensive in order to be faithful? It is surely not a mark of spiritual strength to be intolerant with those who cannot see things from our point of view, and especially to say harsh and cutting things to or about those who, in doctrine and experience, do not measure up to our standard.

We are to "earnestly contend for the faith... " (Jude 3), and we must do it wherever it is so required, but there is one thing even more essential, and that is the manifestation of the holy life. I am content to leave the *skinning*, as some folks have chosen to call it, to those with less concern to be Christlike in their attitudes and kind in their utterances. The harsh, the coarse, the vulgar, the unrefined has no place in the life and service of those who are praying:

"Let the beauty of Jesus be seen in me!"

It demanded a Sacrificial Devotion.

The passage, Romans 12:1, 2, was given to me at the altar as a basis for my consecration. I was to give all I had in consecration, right there, and God would honor it. I did my part, and God faithfully did His.

Soon, however, I discovered that this *living sacrifice* was much more than an altar presentation. It was a life. I was to live at the point of sacrifice! That is God's minimum demand in the sanctified experience, and there is something exquisite about it. It is not merely an experience to preach about, but to embrace.

It demanded an Implicit Obedience.

I found that in taking possession of my life, the Holy One became absolute Master. It was immediately His prerogative to lead and direct. His presence was not always apparent. I was perplexed at first by His strange silences, but soon I learned the difference between a spiritual stillness and a carnal stagnation. There were times when He would prompt and urge, and times when He would restrain. Sometimes He would definitely direct, and sometimes He would seem to leave the choice to me. I found that as I understood the divine will, He demanded immediate obedience, but until I understood it, He would patiently wait.

Sometimes the powers of darkness have sought to confuse the issue by rush tactics, and sometimes they have sought to delay action by satanic interference, but insofar as there has been a quiet, alert, waiting attitude, God's will has always been made clear.

That obedience is demanded yet. He will allow no argument, He insists on being obeyed.

Section II

HERE IS MY DOCTRINE

"The things which become sound doctrine." Titus 2:1.

"That the man of God may be perfect, thoroughly furnished unto all good works." 2 Timothy 3:17.

1
How The Doctrine Unfolded

IT IS ONE THING to receive and enjoy the Blessing of which I have here spoken, but it is another thing altogether to be able to explain the experience to others.

Many people go *heart first* into the sin-cleansing fountain—the *head* follows later. In other words, we first receive the *experience*, then begin to learn its theology and to understand its implications.

From that first night on which God sanctified me wholly, I began to tell it out in definite testimony. So wonderful was the work which He had wrought, I felt I must testify concerning it. I began to tell it in expressions such as these:

> "Thank God, He has sanctified me wholly"; "He has baptized me with the Holy Ghost and fire"; "He has come to dwell in me, delivering me from inbred sin"; and so forth.

It has been my joy through the years that I have never had cause to modify that testimony, to trim the corners or to tone down the declaration I then made, and after the passing of three and a half decades, I am no less certain that my early affirmation was the truth of God. I soon found, however, that if I was to be of lasting help to those to whom

I spoke, it would be necessary to do more than to perpetually repeat my testimony. Some clear explanatory statements were needed, and consequently some definite background work must be done. I also found that, precious to my own heart as the truth had become, it was not welcomed by many whom I had expected to receive it. Some began to talk about the *suppression* of the carnal nature; others insisted that it was more correct to speak of a *continual counteraction* by the indwelling Holy Ghost. Many of my old friends quite bluntly declared that since we were all human and always would be as long as we lived, we must of necessity sin in thought, word and deed all the days of our lives. This vile body was a heavy weight hanging about us, and from it there was no release until God in His mercy should call us Home.

I was warned that I had been deceived; that I was running into fanaticism, that being young, and consequently lacking in judgment, I was not able to discern between truth and error, and had no idea as to the trap into which I had fallen. It became evident, therefore, that if I was to be listened to with any degree of serious consideration, I must be able to give a reason for the hope that was in me—and a scriptural reason, too.

Further, I determined at all costs to preach this truth and desired to find the best possible manner in which to present it. I saw, therefore, that if I was to make progress in this holy way, four things were deeply essential.

I must *know* God in an ever deepening sense through the medium of prayer. I must also *know my Bible* and know it thoroughly through the medium of firsthand consecutive study. I must further know *what other people had written* on this subject, both for and against it, through the ages. And finally, I needed *fellowship,* and therefore must seek friendship with those of a kindred spirit.

I began to follow a definite system of Bible study.

Certainly much Scripture had been given me by those who had led me into this experience, but I determined to be an independent searcher, examining the Word of God for myself. I wanted to read with honesty and candor, not only the Scripture passages which had been given me in support of the doctrine, but also those pointed out by my other friends who said that they were contrary to the holiness interpretation. I determined to know exactly, so far as I was then able, what all these passages really *said*, and what they really meant.

I therefore began to read my Bible in a new way. Starting in the book of Genesis and reading carefully, I traced this subject from cover to cover. Using a colored pencil, I marked the passages wherever I found them—whether they were seemingly for this teaching or against it. As I examined each passage I carefully noted the context, and sought to understand the historic setting. With the use of lexicons I began to examine the important words of the passages—and these through the years have received fuller attention. I gave careful study to the much heralded *opposite passages* as my friends had called them, not neglecting that prime favorite, "If we say that we have no sin, we deceive ourselves, and the truth is not in us." 1 John 1:8.

This study, of course, was a matter of years, but what precious years they were, and when it was concluded I began again, and again, each time using some different method of approach. I am in that study still, and am enjoying it more and more every day. There are so many angles to this thing. How thrilling it is to notice holiness as it relates itself to the various dispensations; as it is seen in the various characters; as it relates itself to the other Bible doctrines, and so to go on and on. There is no end to it.

I was determined at all cost that my investigation should be honest, and that its results should be faithfully proclaimed. Since those early days I have had opportunity to acquire general knowledge which at first I did not possess and whatever has been acquired has been used with a sincere desire more clearly to comprehend divine truth. My conclusion *then* was one which I have since found no reason to modify, namely: The entire Bible from cover to cover has one grand supreme message which is this:—It is the purpose of God in this life to deliver those who can trust Him, from the corruption of indwelling sin. There is not one passage from beginning to end, if read in the light of its context and historical setting, which does not unite to teach either the *need*, the *possibility*, or the *possession* of this experience of Full Salvation.

Also I began to cultivate the habit of reading.

I sought to acquaint myself with all the holiness writers I could find, and also to get a clear conception of other points of view.

Through the years I have steadfastly refused to condemn any teaching as erroneous merely on the tirades of its critics. I have felt that I owed it to any *man* or *movement* against whom error has been charged, to make fullest investigation before uttering my condemnation. Prejudice as the result of hearsay has done more damage than we can conceive.

The result of my search has been a continued confirmation of my own experience. I have read many arguments against it and many denunciations of it which had neither logic nor argument. Scripture has been used, usually misused, verses being misquoted, misinterpreted and wrenched from their context, but in no case have I found any reasoned argument based on sound Scripture interpretation which has weakened the position I took when in response to a confession of my inward depravity and the complete consecration I then made, God by that fiery baptism performed within me His sin-consuming work.

> "To all the world I dare avow
> That Jesus sanctifies me now!"

I sought fellowship with others who were walking this Holy Way.

My experience through the years has confirmed me in the view that one of the fruitful causes of difficulty among those who desire this experience is the lack of suitable fellowship. It soon dawned on me that the fact that God had sanctified me wholly was only part of the blessing I had received: He had given me *"inheritance among all them which are sanctified."* Acts 20:32.

That consciousness soon meant everything to me. How I delighted in those early fellowships. The man with the shining face took me for long walks in the fields, gave me spiritual instruction, encouraged me, helped me to pray and sought to build me up in my most holy faith. I cannot even estimate my indebtedness under God to the enlightenment received through his instrumentality.

Around me also were a number of praying men, members of the League of Prayer, which had organized the convention in which God sanctified me. They loved to pray, and soon I caught their passion. Frequent nights were set apart for all nights of prayer, and the victories won there on our knees will be a record to be read when the triumphs of grace are reviewed in the world to come. Some of these men were giants. They helped me in my early walk with God.

Among my earliest acquaintances also was Rev. Thomas Cook, then president of Cliff College. Out of his big heart he invited me to visit Cliff for prayer and consultation. And how Thomas Cook could pray. Here was another man whose face shone. In his biography written by his brother, the story is told of an incident aboard an Atlantic liner while making one of his several preaching tours to the United States. Opening a door on the ship's deck, he discovered he had inadvertently gone to the smoke room, and after standing in the doorway a little while, he closed the door and went his way. While he stood there, however, every man took his pipe from his lips and dropped his cards. After Mr. Cook had left, one of the men turned to his friend and said, "Say, why did we drop our pipes and cards when that fellow appeared?" In a subdued voice his friend replied, "Who could smoke and play cards in the presence of a face like that?" To know Mr. Cook was to get the immediate answer to the question. He walked with God.

Mr. Cook's colleague and successor, Rev. Samuel Chadwick, was another stalwart whose friendship I prized and whose memory is a treasured possession. He hated fanaticism, loathed pretense and was the sworn foe of petty criticism. He stood unflinchingly for this great truth. My more intimate contacts with him were during the last ten years of his life, when as speaker at the Southport Convention of which he was president, and visiting lecturer to Cliff College, I got really close to his heart. Some of my most precious memories have to do with the midnight talks as we sat in his study beside that log fire which he loved so much, and talked about the things of God. After these talks he would write his weekly *Joyful News* article. Since his death, these articles which were often written in series, have been gathered into book form, under such now familiar titles as "The Way of the Cross," "The Path of Prayer," "The Way to Pentecost," "The Call to Perfection." The only book he published was a book of sermons, "Humanity and God." It is now out of print.

In those after-midnight hours he would ponder over the Scriptures until they talked to him and opened up the choicest secrets to his heart. When some new light broke, he became almost excited about it, and when he got it, it was something to get excited about. I remember one morning, walking into his study after having left him in meditation the night before, and as soon as I entered, he looked up with a sparkle in his eye and said, "Jessop, I have just had a rare find; look what the Lord says here!"

When the Book began to glow before the eyes of Samuel

Chadwick, he made no apologies for calling it "What the Lord says."

He appreciated a straight holiness message, and nothing I ever heard or said about the destruction of the *old man* was too rigid for him to enjoy. I remember after one of my Southport Convention addresses he rose and said, "Brother Jessop is right; it is the purpose of God that the body of sin should be *destroyed*," and the emphasis he placed on that last word left no doubt as to what he meant.

Many others helped me in the development of my doctrine, but only one more name can here be mentioned, that of David Thomas.

For a number of years after the night he preached on which I entered into Blessing, I lost sight of him, and then one day God providentially again brought him into my life. By this time he had founded the International Holiness Mission and had become its first president, while I had entered the ministry and was pastor of a Baptist Church. A Baptist minister preaching holiness! I know, of course, that this may not be common, but a Baptist is not necessarily a Calvinist. I preached holiness and God honored it.

David Thomas heard me preach in a holiness convention and invited me to join him in the work of the International Holiness Mission. While by that time my doctrine was well established, one of the privileges of working with David Thomas was the encouragement received in the matter of expression.

He reveled in the thought of the destruction of *the old man*. No man could work with David Thomas through those twelve years without being so thoroughly drilled in certainty of expression that everybody knew what he meant.

2
Into What This Crystallized

Through the years there has come increasing light, expansion and development, but the clearer the truth has become, the more confident have I been that my doctrine is broad-based on the Word of God, and my experience is deeply inwrought by the Holy Ghost.

For the sake of clarity I shall state as concisely as possible the doctrinal position and then take up some things by way of explanation.

(1)
The Doctrinal Position

That position is exceedingly simple and is *very* old-fashioned — so old-fashioned indeed that to the modern mind it will appear to be hopelessly out of date. Concerning it, a threefold statement will suffice.

As to Man's Natural Condition.

Apart from saving grace man is hopelessly lost; his "sinnerhood" is beyond dispute. By reason of racial inheritance he finds within himself a depraved disposition, and by personal participation he ratifies his "sinnerhood" and seals his condemnation. Psalm 51:5; Romans 7:17; Ephesians

2:3; Mark 7:21, 23; Romans 3:12, 23.

As to the Sinner's Hope of Salvation.

Approaching God through the Calvary merits of His Son by the pathway of repentance and faith, he asks and obtains a full and free forgiveness, is born into the family of God, and receives the Spirit's witness to this transaction within his soul.

a. *The past is fully dealt with*—he is justified freely. The law finds nothing with which to change him. "Being justified freely by his grace through the redemption that is in Christ Jesus." Romans 3:24.

b. *A new life is imparted*—The very life of God Himself. The world has now nothing with which to satisfy him. "Being born again, not of corruptible seed, but of incorruptible, by the Word of God, which liveth and abideth forever." 1 Peter 1:23; John 1:12, 13; 3:1-18.

c. *An unmistakable assurance is implanted*—the witness of the Holy Spirit. The powers of hell cannot gainsay him. Romans 8:15, 16.

The soul really born again is saved and knows it. He has passed from death unto life. John 5:24; 1 John 5:13.

As to the Believer's Privilege of Sanctification.

It is the inestimable privilege of the believing soul to be sanctified wholly. 1 Thessalonians 5:22, 23.

This is accomplished through:

a. On the human side:

A complete consecration. Romans 12:1, 2; 1 Corinthians 6:19, 20; 2 Corinthians 8:5.

An appropriating faith. Acts 26:18.

b. On the divine side:

The baptism with the Holy Ghost and fire. Matthew 3:11.

The preliminary conditions are:

a. A conscious sense of need. Isaiah 6:5; Psalm 51:1-6; Matthew 5:6.

b. A candid confession of that need. Isaiah 6:5; Psalm 51:1-6.

c. A removal of every known hindrance and the utter renunciation of every evil thing. Matthew 5:23, 24; Acts 5:3.

The Results Produced are:
    a. Purification of the heart. Acts 15:8, 9; Matthew 5:8.
    b. Power for consecrated service. Acts 1:8.
    c. An increased spiritual fullness. Acts 2:4; Ephesians 5:18.
    d. A progressive life in God. Ephesians 3:14-21.[1]

(2)
A Necessary Explanation

In making this doctrinal statement it is important that we should be explicit in our explanation concerning some of the words and expressions used by the Holiness People. If our critics are honest they will be eager to find our thought content when these words are used and they will steadfastly refuse to interpret them or allow others to interpret them in any other way.

The chief offending words seem to be, *sanctify, holy, and perfect*; while the outstanding difficulties are evidently the distinction between the *human* and the *carnal*, and the possibility of a complete deliverance from indwelling sin in this life.

a. *The words "sanctify" and "holy"—their twofold meaning.*

Every careful student of Scripture is aware that its great doctrines are revealed by a careful development of thought as the human mind is capable of receiving them. No doctrine is given to us *ready-made*. God had first to prepare a people to become the vehicle of truth, and He took them as we would take a class of children, developing ideas by means of pictures; picture words, pictorial events, types, shadows,

---

1. For a fuller discussion of this subject see *Foundations of Doctrine in Scripture and Experience*, a textbook used in Bible Schools and Colleges. Now [1941] in its third edition.

adumbrations; all with one aim in view— preparation for the fuller revelation yet to come.

A study of these words *sanctify* and *holy* will reveal such a development. The Old Testament idea is that of *separation*. There, in many cases the question of moral content does not enter in at all; the separation is purely legal and ceremonial. People, places, and even inanimate objects are sanctified. Men sanctify themselves and are commanded to sanctify each other. What was thus *sanctified* was regarded as *holy*, not because of any moral quality but because it was *set apart* for holy purposes.

In the New Testament things alter. Not that the separation idea is abandoned; it is rather expanded and given a fuller thought content, being made to include purification, the *ceremonial* giving place to the *moral*, Calvary and Pentecost making the difference.[2]

In some places the separation idea alone is seen, while in others the thought of purification is apparent. In one significant passage, John 17:17-19, both thoughts are indicated, one concerning the Lord and the other concerning His people. In each case the context will help the reader to decide the meaning.

There is surely a difference between "them that are sanctified in Christ Jesus, called to be saints," 1 Corinthians 1:2, and "The very God of peace sanctify you wholly," 1 Thessalonians 5:23; also, "And I, brethren, could not speak unto you as unto *spiritual*, but as unto *carnal*, even as unto babes in Christ." 1 Corinthians 3:1.

These *carnal* Christians were *sanctified* in the sense of separation between Christian profession and the world, but they were badly in need of purification as the rest of the epistle will show; in fact, there were those among them who, if they had ever known anything of saving grace, were now a long way from it.

---

2. For a fuller discussion of this thought see *Foundations of Doctrine in Scripture and Experience.* pp. 178-189.]

b. *The word perfect—Its twofold suggestiveness.*

No word has been more abused by the professing people of God than this word *perfect*. Joining it to an adjective with which it is never found in the Word of God, and thus injecting a thought content which is neither intended nor implied, they talk about *sinless perfection* and proceed to prove how impossible such an experience is in this life, and then either ignorantly or maliciously— we must leave God to decide which—they begin to apply their conclusions to the experience of entire sanctification, saying in effect— sinless perfection is not possible in this life; the Holiness People profess to be perfect, therefore, they are in error.

The mistake here made is in overlooking the fact that in using the word *perfect*, our English Bible makes no distinction in its translation of two words which widely differ, one having to do with the end attained by a *process* and never completed here on earth, and the other indicative of adjustment and fitness resulting from a work. One passage of Scripture in which both these words occur will be sufficient to illustrate what we mean:

> "If by any means I might attain unto the resurrection of the dead. Not as though I had already attained, either were already *perfect*: but I follow after... Let us therefore, as many as be *perfect*..." Philippians 3:11, 12-15.

Is it not immediately clear that in this passage the apostle claims one perfection, yet disclaims another? No sane professor of entire sanctification has ever professed the perfection which the apostle here disclaims, but all who enjoy the experience revel in and testify to the experience he here professes, and such an experience is surely not too much to expect.

The wholly sanctified soul claims to have been perfected in a love relationship between the soul and God. This perfection consists in the fulfillment of the purpose for which the soul was designed. Whatever fulfills the purpose for which it is designed is in that sense perfect. A watch, a fountain pen, or anything else is perfect if it does that for which it is made. Man's chief end is to glorify God. The sanctified soul lives for His glory. In the wider sense that soul is in the perfecting process of ever deepening conformity to the image of its Lord. It will be *perfected* when it sees Him face to face.[3]

c. *The words* HUMAN *and* CARNAL—*their necessary distinction.*

There has been more confusion here than many imagine. In so many minds the old gnostic idea that the body is inherently sinful, has so firmly entrenched itself that men and women have come to believe that there is no hope of deliverance from indwelling sin so long as they live in a body of flesh and blood. They fail to see the difference between the *weakness* of the human and the *wickedness* of the carnal.

Both of these stand related to the Calvary work of Jesus. The *human* is to be cleansed and divinely possessed, while the *carnal* is to be destroyed. Romans 6:6; 1 John 1:9.[4]

There are many other distinctions which the soul walking in the light will learn to recognize, but with which we have no further space to deal. The interested reader is recommended to take up a study of the book, *Foundations of Doctrine in Scripture and Experience,* where a full discussion of the subject will be found.

Our Lord taught the necessity and possibility of heart holiness. Paul and other New Testament writers expanded and emphasized this truth.

John and Charles Wesley with their eighteenth century colleagues, and the many who through the years have been graciously led into this experience, have rejoiced to publish it.

3. For a fuller discussion of this thought see *Foundations of Doctrine in Scripture and Experience.* pp. 159-177.

4. For a fuller discussion of this thought see *Foundations of Doctrine in Scripture and Experience.* pp. 116-134.

We conclude with John Wesley's oft quoted and memorable words:

"In 1729 my brother Charles and I, reading the Bible, and seeing we could not be saved without holiness, followed after it, and incited others to do so. In 1737 we saw that holiness comes by faith. In 1738 we saw that men are justified before they are sanctified; but still holiness was our pursuit—inward and outward holiness. God then thrust us out to raise up a holy people."

Early Methodism became the source of the modern Holiness Movement, and so the truth goes forward.

> "More and more it spreads and grows
>   Ever mighty to prevail;
> Sin's stronghold it now o'erthrows,
>   Shakes the trembling gates of hell."

Section III

THESE ARE MY PEOPLE

"Inheritance among them which are sanctified by faith..."
Acts 26:18.

From the moment that God sanctified me wholly, the Holiness People were my people. As a people, they are by no means free from human weaknesses—the best among them would acknowledge that; yet to know them is to love them. They are the salt of the earth; the very finest people I know. I have seen them under varying circumstances and in many places, but never once did I have reason to regret my association with them.

Here, however, it might be well to identify these people, especially in view of some mistaken ideas and at times we fear *misrepresentation,* which are circulated concerning them. Some necessary distinctions must be made if we are to understand the Holiness Movement aright.

1
We Must Distinguish Between the Holiness People— and Some Who Have Been Mistakenly Identified With Them.

IT IS NOT UNCOMMON for persons uninstructed here to make sweeping statements which, when in possession of more accurate knowledge, they find it necessary to modify. The following will indicate what I mean. Some time ago an article appeared in a religious periodical with this blatant caption: *Nuts for the Holiness Sect to Crack.*

As I read it, two things were immediately apparent. First, it was evident that the writer did not know the Holiness People; he had no acquaintance with them and had no idea as to who they were. Further, it was equally evident that he had no knowledge whatsoever as to what the Holiness People taught. At any rate it is certain that on reading what was said about them, the Holiness People would not have recognized themselves.

After some thought and prayer I wrote this man a brotherly letter concerning both the *nuts* and the *sect* and on receiving his reply, I discovered exactly what I had suspected; he had been attacking one thing and naming another. I wrote to a seeming antagonist, but found only a befogged mind needing help.

At this point it will be well to notice two important facts which need to be clearly understood.

a. *The Holiness Movement is not a "sect."*

Certainly of late years there have come into being certain denominational churches whose major emphasis is declared to be the doctrine of Scriptural Holiness. Through the centuries churches have arisen declaring this truth, as did the Methodist Church and others after it. Some have become silent on their witness, others have become extinct, but the Holiness Movement remains. It is not limited to churches; they are rather the product of it. This great spiritual experience is bigger than churches, and certainly could not be confined within a *sect*. It transcends all denominational barriers and knows no national boundaries. It is a deep spiritual bond—far too deep to be affected by surface things, concerning only kindred souls baptized into one body by the Spirit of God.

b. *The Holiness Movement has recognized Limitations.*

Of these, two at least should be noted:

As to doctrinal emphasis.

It knows nothing of suppression, counteraction, continual re-consecration, daily dying, and the like, so far as indwelling sin is concerned, but on the contrary it stresses a complete, perfect and instantaneous deliverance from inward depravity.

As to recognized adherents.

It knows nothing of modern Pentecostalism, so called, and repudiates with emphasis those coarse and vulgar exercises where misguided souls roll, scream and chatter. Its adherents are sane and sensible folk whose chief concern is the experience of a pure heart, received and retained through obedient faith.

2

We Must Distinguish Between the Holiness People— and Some Who Have Unfortunately Attached Themselves to Them.

IT IS RECORDED that when Israel left Egypt for the promised land, "a mixed multitude also went up with them." Exodus 12:38. That *mixed multitude* was *with* them, but not *of* them, and was responsible for no end of trouble. It would hardly have been fair to Israel to judge them at their *best* by this mixture at its *worst*; no reasonable person would have done that.

It is also true that around every modern movement an encircling *mixed multitude* exists. They are around it, yet not part of it and in time of crisis would scatter from it. It is not surprising, therefore, that the Holiness Movement should experience something of that nature; there has been a *mixed multitude* around it which has not always been of the greatest help.

These *out-on-the-fringe people* have associated with us for various reasons. Some were attracted by the measure of freedom manifested in our services; others are interested in investigating our doctrines. After a while they will be investigating the doctrines of the Calvinists, and after that the doctrines of Christian Science, then perhaps the doctrines of Spiritism or Jehovah's Witnesses, or something else. They are no more part of us than of any other crowd around which they circle. Some are around us because no one else would tolerate them. That they do not enhance our reputation, we are fully aware, but since the Lord whom we serve "came into the world to save sinners," it would ill become us to turn such people away.

That some have even professed the experience of Full Salvation and in glib tones have talked about things which to us are sacred without any corresponding inward knowledge is also true.

Yet all these are no more part of the real Holiness Movement than a bird is part of a tree if it happens to make its nest therein. It is by no means to the discredit of the tree that an undesirable bird has lodged in its branches.

3

WE MUST DISTINGUISH BETWEEN THE HOLINESS PEOPLE— AND WHAT HAS BEEN MALICIOUSLY SAID ABOUT THEM.

THE ATTACKS MADE on the Holiness Movement has been both numerous and venomous, and had it not been that the Movement and its teaching were of God, they would surely have been crushed long ago. The tragedy of all this, however, is the source from which these attacks have come; professing servants of God with Bible in hand, being the worst offenders.

It is neither safe nor fair to evaluate any movement or any individual from the utterances of their critics. Few critics have enough *grace* to content themselves with plain, unbiased statements as to proven facts; even if they hold to the bare truth, usually it is so *bare* that it has been stripped of the necessary explanations which would make it clear to the uninformed mind, or else on the other hand, it is clothed with an emphasis which is sufficient to make it misleading. The man who does this, whatever may be his position, is guilty of foul treachery with regard to truth, and is unworthy of a place of leadership in the Christian church.

The most obvious thing about these attacks is their parrot-like nature. They are repeated over and over with an air of wisdom deceiving to the beginner, leading him to believe that they are ideas newly born, whereas they have been parroted and parroted until it would seem that those who uttered them would be ashamed ever again to look a self-respecting parrot in the face, yet through the years this amazing repetition goes on. In beginners it is excusable—they say what they are taught to say—but in men of riper years it is abominable, evidencing very clearly one of two things: either they have never carefully considered the subject, and therefore are guilty of attacking something they have not taken time and pains to understand, or else they do understand and have set themselves deliberately to misrepresent it. In either case the action is equally culpable.

The attacks have been far too numerable to allow any attempt at a detailed answer here.[1] They may be grouped under limited heads and stated as follows:

a. *The Perfection Bogey.*

How often has it been flung out—and with a sting that has been anything but gracious—"The holiness people and their teaching of sinless perfection."

Our observation is, we have now been among the Holiness People for thirty-five years, but we have never heard this teaching, nor have we read of any accredited leader among them having taught it. We would, therefore, like to put this question to all who make such a charge, a question we have asked again and again, never to obtain a satisfactory answer. Will you please tell us *who* among the Holiness People does preach or teach *Sinless Perfection*? Tell us *who* did it, *where* he did it, and just *what* he said.

The charge, "They teach… ," is far too nebulous.

Who are *they*? If *they* do teach this thing, there must be a localized voice among them somewhere that is doing it, and

1. These objections to second Blessing Holiness are taken up in full and frank discussion in *Foundations of Doctrine in Scripture and Experience*, pp. 199-200.]

there must be some very definite sentences in which the teaching is being couched. We want to know. Please name the man and the pulpit, or the book or periodical.

A sinless perfectionist—meaning of course one teaching that he is no longer liable to sin and is beyond making any further mistakes—would have an interesting time among the Holiness People I know.

b. *The Pharisee Scarecrow.*

Says one of the opponents of this truth, "The profession of holiness is often the veriest pharisaism."

Here again is one of those very general statements which *slurs* everybody, but *charges* nobody, and is utterly unworthy of Christian leadership. It is one of those statements with which it is impossible to deal, as that writer well knew when he made it.

For us to say that none of the pharisee element ever associated itself with the Holiness Movement would, of course, be an unwarrantable assertion. We wonder whether there has ever been at any time any great Christian truth that has not been professedly embraced by some whose lives have not adorned it? Would our Calvinistic friends be prepared to state that all who declare that they are eternally saved through the Redeemer's finished work, are creditable adherents to that teaching? Personally, of course, we do not endorse such teaching, but we have had enough experience to know that our friends who hold and teach it cannot be made responsible for those who abuse it. If its falsity is to be established, and we are persuaded that it may be, it must be on scriptural grounds; on no account must there be recourse to the slinging of mud, which would besmear any, who despite their error, may be precious children of God.

To attack any doctrine on the ground of the charged unfaithfulness of professed adherents is unsound in method, and as to the logic of the argument, we leave the reader to judge.

But that is not the end of this thing. We must now ask by what authority is this verdict of *veriest pharisaism* given? Who are these people who are so charged? Where do they live? By what standard are they pharisaic? Is it a standard or is it somebody's notion? And who is this man who dares to apply this measurement? By whose appointment does he occupy this exalted office?

"The profession of holiness is often the veriest pharisaism." It will be interesting to call the roll of some of these pharisees and let them in their own words give their response. Here are some:

Jesus:

God's own Son; The World's Saviour; The Church's Lord; The Founder of the Holiness Movement. Lord Jesus, will you make a statement?

"Blessed are the pure in heart, for they shall see God." Matthew 5:8. Evidently there are such people.

Paul:

Missionary and Apostle! What have you to say?

"Let us therefore, as many as be perfect, be thus minded." Philippians 3:15

Peter:

Apostle; representative to the Jerusalem Conference. What is your testimony?

"And God, which knoweth the hearts, bear them witness, giving them the Holy Ghost, even as He did unto us; and put no difference between us and them, purifying their hearts by faith." Acts 15:8, 9.

John Wesley:

The evangelist whose preaching saved England from revolution, and became the basis of the world's largest evangelical church.

Mr. Wesley, will you please give us your reply to this charge of veriest pharisaism? Did you ever profess this experience?

"Many years since, I saw that without holiness no man shall see the Lord. I began to follow after it, and inciting all with whom I had any personal intercourse to do the same. Ten years after, God gave me a clearer view than I had before of the way to attain this; namely by faith in the Son of God. And immediately I declared to all, 'we are saved from all sin, we are made holy by faith.' This I testified in private, in public, in print; and God confirmed it by a thousand witnesses. I have continued to declare this for about thirty years and God has continued to confirm the words by His grace." — *Wesley's Works*.

Adam Clarke:

Methodist Scholar and Commentator. One of the foremost scholars of his day.

Dr. Clarke, your testimony, please.

"I regarded nothing, not even life itself, in comparison with having my heart cleansed from all sin, and began to seek it with full purpose of heart. Soon after this, while earnestly wrestling with the Lord in prayer… I found a change wrought within my soul which I have endeavored through grace to maintain amid the grievous temptations and accusations of the subtle foe."

John Fletcher:

Vicar of Madeley, Shropshire, England. Author of among other works, *Checks to Antinomianism*.

Mr. Fletcher, what do you have to say?

"I will confess Him to all the world, and I declare unto you, in the presence of God the Holy Trinity, I am now dead indeed unto sin. I do not say 'I am crucified with Christ' because some of our well-meaning brethren say, 'By this can only be meant a gradual dying'; but I profess unto you that I am dead unto sin and alive unto God. He is my Prophet, Priest and King, my indwelling holiness; my all in all." — *In Journal of Hester Ann Rogers*, p. 136.

T. C. Upham:

Professor of Mental and Moral Philosophy, Author of *The Principles of the Interior or Hidden Life.*

Dr. Upham, your testimony, please:

"I was distinctly conscious when I reached it. The selfish exercises which had recently, and as it were, by a concentrated and spasmodic effort, troubled me so much, seemed to be at once removed; and I believed, and had reason to believe that my heart, presumptuous as it may appear to some to say it, was now purified by the Holy Spirit.... I was thus... filled with the blessing of perfect love."

Frances E. Willard:

Temperance Reformer and Educator.

Miss Willard, will you say something.

"I began to desire and pray for holiness of heart kneeling in utter abandonment I consecrated myself anew to God... I unconditionally yielded my pretty little jewels, and great peace came to my soul. I cannot describe the deep welling up of joy that gradually possessed me. The conscious emotional presence of Christ through the Holy Spirit held me. All my friends knew and noticed the change... I was shut in with my Lord."

Daniel Steele, D.D.:

Professor in Boston University.

Dr. Steele, will you testify?

"I was led by the study of the promised Paraclete to see that He signified far more than I had realized in the new birth and that a personal pentecost was awaiting me. I sought in downright earnestness. Then the Spirit uncovered to my gaze the evil still lurking in my nature; the mixed motives with which I had preached, often preferring the honor which comes from men to that which comes from God. I submitted to every test presented by the Holy Spirit and publicly confessed what He had revealed, and determined to walk with God rather than with the multitude in the world or in the church… Upon the promise I ventured with an act of appropriating faith, claiming the Comforter as my right in the name of Jesus. For several hours I clung by naked faith, praying and repeating Charles Wesley's hymn:

> "Jesus, thine all victorious love
> Shed in *my* heart abroad."

"Suddenly I became conscious of a mysterious power exerting itself on my sensibilities… as if an electric current were passing through my body with painless shocks, melting my whole being into a fiery stream of love… I did not at first realize that this was entire sanctification. The positive part of my experience had eclipsed the negative, the elimination of the sin principle by the cleansing power of the Paraclete."

Asa Mahan, L.L.D:
President of Oberlin College.
Dr. Mahan, your testimony, please.
"On Sabbath, November 9, 1884, I completed the eighty-fifth year of my life. The first seventeen years of that period were spent in the darkness and impenitence of sin. The following eighteen years I lived in the dim twilight of semi-faith which fully knows Christ in the sphere of *Justification by faith* but knows almost nothing of Him in the sphere of *sanctification by faith* and is absolutely ignorant of Him in the promise, 'He shall baptize you with the Holy Ghost and with fire.'

"During the subsequent fifty years I have found grace to walk with God in the sphere of cloudless sunlight in which we are *complete in Christ* and know Him as our wisdom, righteousness, sanctification and redemption; know Him not only as the Lamb of God which taketh away the sin of the world, but as 'He which baptizeth with the Holy Ghost,' and in which, consequently, God is our everlasting light, and the days of our mourning are ended.

"When I apprehended that He was just as able to *sanctify me* wholly as to justify me fully, then, totally renouncing self and self dependence, I entered upon the life of faith in its true and proper form… As a result of fifty years experience and careful self watchfulness, I present myself as a witness for Christ, that 'our old man' may be 'crucified with Him' and 'the body of sin destroyed that henceforth we should not serve sin.'"

Frances Ridley Havergal:

Well-known writer of devotional hymns.

Miss Havergal, do you have anything to say?

"It was on Advent Sunday, December 2, 1873, I first saw clearly the blessedness of consecration. I saw it as a flash of electric light, and what you *see* you can never *unsee*… First I was shown that 'the blood of Jesus Christ His Son cleanseth us from *all sin*.' And then it was made plain to me that He who had thus cleansed me had power to keep me clean; so I just utterly yielded myself to Him and simply trusted Him to keep me."

Samuel Logan Brengle:

Commissioner in Salvation Army.

Commissioner, give us your testimony.

"It was a heaven of love that came into my heart. My soul melted like wax before fire. I loathed myself that I had ever sinned against Him or doubted Him, or lived for myself and not for His glory. Every ambition for self was now gall; the pure flame of love burned it like a blazing fire would burn a moth. I walked out over Boston Commons before breakfast weeping for joy and praising God. Oh, how I loved! In that hour I knew Jesus, and I loved Him till it seemed my heart would burst with love. I was filled with love for all His creatures. I heard the little sparrows chattering; I loved them. I saw a little worm wiggling across my path; I stepped over it; I didn't want to hurt any living thing. I loved the dogs, I loved the horses, I loved the little urchins on the street, I loved the strangers who hurried past me, I loved the heathen—I loved the whole world.

"I have never doubted this experience since. It was a living experience. In time God withdrew something of those tremendous emotional feelings. He taught me that I had to live by faith and not by my emotions. I walked in a blaze of glory for weeks, but the glory subsided, and He made me see that I must walk and run instead of mounting up with wings. He showed me that I must learn to trust Him, to have confidence in His unfailing love and devotion regardless of how I felt… "

Thomas Cook:

Methodist Connectional Evangelist. Then first Methodist President of Cliff College, England.

Mr. Cook, what is your word of witness?

"My conversion was so clear and satisfactory that I can never doubt its reality. The beginnings of this life of loyalty and love I shall never forget… With such experiences, is there any wonder that I imagined the work of moral renovation was perfected, that sin was not only forgiven but fully expelled from my soul? But soon I discovered my mistake. My highly wrought emotions subsided, and petty annoyances of life chafed, the temptations of the devil assailed; and then I found out as pride, envy, unbelief, selfwill, and other forms of heart sin stirred within me, that much needed to be done before I could be 'meet for the inheritance of the saints in light'… My experience was full of fits and starts, changeable, and uneven. I was conscious also of a mighty want; there was a vacuum in my nature which grace had not filled, a strange sense of need which I cannot describe, but which all who love the Lord Jesus with less than perfect love will understand…

"For three years this half and half sort of life continued, when I was so dissatisfied that I felt unless I had something better I could not go on longer... I began at once to seek it, determined to give God no rest until I was sanctified wholly...

"Some months passed during which time I was almost in a state of despair; but my extremity was God's opportunity. At this very juncture, when I felt I must die unless I received the grace, an evangelist came to our town and proclaimed 'full salvation' to be a present duty and privilege. There was no disputing his teaching; if by faith, it must be a present experience. Faith cannot be otherwise than an instantaneous operation. It was like a revelation from heaven to me.

"The passage, 'If we walk in the light as he is in the light, we have fellowship one with another and the blood of Jesus Christ his Son cleanseth us from all sin,' was instantly applied to my heart with such power as I had never felt before. What a fullness of meaning I saw in the words. Was I walking in the light? Truthfully I could answer, 'Yes, Lord; so far as I know I am doing Thy will, and will do it, by Thy grace helping me.' I saw then that the passage was not so much a promise as a plain declaration. If I walked in the light, the full cleansing from sin was my heritage, and all I had to do was to immediately claim. Without a moment's hesitation I did so, and cried out at the top of my voice, 'I claim the Blessing now.' My friends then began to sing:

> ''Tis done! Thou dost this moment save,
> With full salvation bless;
> Redemption through thy blood I have,
> And spotless love and peace.'

"While they sang, the refining fire came down and went through my heart, searching, melting, burning, filling all its chambers with light, and hallowing my whole being to God."—*New Testament Holiness,* pp. 197-206.

Samuel Chadwick, D.D.:

Second Methodist President of Cliff College.

Dr. Chadwick, won't you tell us about this experience?

"I owe everything to the gift of Pentecost… When it came I could not explain what had happened, but I was aware of things unspeakable and full of glory…

"Holiness does not come by growth… Holiness implies a crisis, a new experience, a transformed life. It is not an achievement, or an attainment, but a gift of grace in the Holy Ghost. It is by faith. It is as distinctly a second work of grace as regeneration is a new birth. Consecration is as practical as repentance and sanctification as regeneration. Unbelief stumbles at a name and the heart shrinks from a crisis which involves a death and a resurrection. Satan multiplies difficulties and an evil heart backs him…

"The Spirit of Holiness makes the heart clean… The blessing I sought was power. The blessing God gave began farther in and deeper down. Power was conditioned. The truth that sanctifies begins with the cleansing of the heart." — *The Way to Pentecost*, pp. 87, 88, 123.

Dwight L. Moody:

World evangelist and mighty soul winner.

Mr. Moody, do you have a testimony to a Second Work of Grace?

"The Blessing came upon me suddenly, like a flash of lightning. For months I had been hungering and thirsting for power for service. I had come to that point that I think I would have died if I had not got it. I remember I was walking the streets of New York. I had no more heart in the business I was about than if I had not belonged to this world at all. Right there, on the street, the power of God seemed to come upon me so wonderfully that I had to ask God to stay His hand. I was filled with a sense of God's goodness, and felt as though I could take the world to my heart. I took the old sermon that I had before without any power;

it was the same old truth, but there was a new power. Many were impressed and converted. This happened years after I was converted myself...

"Since then I have never lost the assurance that I am walking in communion with God, and I have a joy in His service that sustains me and makes it easy work. I believe I was an older man than I am now; I have been growing younger ever since." — *The Christian*, London, 1886. Also *Forty Witnesses*.

All these witnesses are outstanding for their notoriety. To them could be added many others just as famous, and thousands not so well known.

c. *The* PECULIARITY SLUR.

With an air of superiority some have endeavored to belittle the Holiness Movement by the slur they cast upon its people. They are peculiar! And very second rate! Take for instance, the following:

"Superstition and fanaticism of the grossest character find a hotbed among *Holiness* advocates. Witness the present disgusting *Tongues Movement* with its attendant delusions and insanities. An unhealthy craving for new and thrilling religious sensations, the emotional meetings of a most exciting character readily account for these things."

It is at least good to know what some people think about us, but again we say, we have grave doubts as to whether those more intimately associated with the Holiness Movement would be able to recognize it from such a description.

It would be to no good purpose, indeed it would not be true for us to deny that within the Holiness Movement there have been, and doubtless now are, some oddities. What movement does not have them? My concern here, however, is the credit so generously given us for the things we do not possess. Our critics are far too generous. Looking around on the many *movements* which, during the past few decades have sprung up within the bounds of Christendom, they have discovered these outcroppings of fanaticism, and seeking to find a place to catalog them, have not been able to think of anything better than to smear the Holiness People by giving them the full credit for them. Perhaps the kindest comment we could make would be to say that any person as manifestly lacking in power to discriminate between things which differ as to make such sweeping statements, would do better service to the cause of truth if his ability were devoted to other themes.

4
WHO THEN ARE THE HOLINESS PEOPLE—
AND WHAT DO THEY TEACH?

HAVING MADE THESE DISTINCTIONS, it will now be necessary to make a definite concluding statement as to who the Holiness People really are, and what they do actually teach.

While as we have seen, in the Old Testament there was a distinctive holiness witness according to the light of the period, the Holiness Movement proper began on the Day of Pentecost when on those waiting representatives of the Christian Church, God sent the Holy Ghost, thereby empowering them for service and purifying their hearts. Acts 1:8; 15:8, 9.

From that time onward there have been periods when the light has been a flame, and seasons when it has almost been a smoking flax, yet God has never allowed it completely to die. The father of the Modern Holiness Movement—using the word *modern* in the best sense—was John Wesley. He it was who coined, or at least sanctioned, the expression, *the Second Blessing*. He discouraged enthusiasm—the word he used for fanaticism and sensationalism—

and preached a sane experience of Bible holiness, received by faith and producing the fruit of the Spirit in daily life. The Holiness Movement is the testimony to this Wesleyan Doctrine as inwrought in individual experience and that testimony is interdenominational and international. Wherever there is a soul sanctified wholly and sanely testifying to it, *there* is the Holiness Movement.

It is to be regretted that within the Christian church the testimony to faith in a sin-destroying Saviour should have brought such dissension and even derision, and that professedly on Biblical grounds.

With a world on fire, it is much too bad that Christians should have no better sense, to say nothing of grace, than to fight each other when unitedly they might fight a common enemy for the glory of God.

As a closing word, I shall repeat what has been reiterated by recognized holiness teachers again and again:

We do *not* teach absolute or sinless perfection. The perfection we teach is derived from the presence of a perfect Saviour, and is that which He commands in the Sermon on the Mount. Matthew 5:48.

We do *not* teach that we can reach an experience where we cannot be tempted, but rather, being tempted we need not fall. Matthew 4:1; 1 Corinthians 10:13.

We do *not* teach that we have reached or can reach a state from which we cannot fall. Hebrews 6:4-6.

We do *not* say we have not sinned or that we cannot sin, but rather that He who is able to keep us from falling, saves us now. Jude 24.

We *do* say that our Lord and Saviour Jesus Christ "gave himself for us, that he might redeem us from all iniquity, and purify unto himself a people for his own possession zealous of good works." Titus 2:14.

Do *you* desire such an experience? The God who "giveth

to all men liberally" is holding it out to you. You may have it *now*. Here are the words of your Lord Himself:

"I say unto you, Ask, and it shall be given you; seek, and ye shall find; knock, and it shall be opened unto you. For every one that asketh receiveth; and he that seeketh findeth; and to him that knocketh it shall be opened.

"If a son shall ask bread of any of you that is a father, will he give him a stone? Or if he ask a fish, will he for a fish give him a serpent? Or if he shall ask an egg, will he offer him a scorpion?

"If ye then, being evil, know how to give good gifts unto your children: how much more shall your heavenly Father give the Holy Spirit to them that ask him?" Luke 11:9-13.

Made in the USA
Monee, IL
07 July 2026